LOOKING BACK
SCHOOL HOME CONNECTION

Dear Family,

In Unit 3 we learned about money, time, graphs, and probability. Here is a game for us to play together. This game will give me a chance to show you what I have learned.

Love,

_____

Directions:
1. Put your game piece at START.
2. Your partner chooses 4 buttons and puts some into each hand.
3. Choose one of your partner's hands. Your partner opens that hand.
4. Count the buttons. Move forward that many spaces.
5. Use coins to show the amount on the price tag with the fewest coins or read the clock and tell the time.
6. Take turns. The first person to get to END is the winner.

Materials:
- 2 game pieces
- buttons
- pennies, nickels, dimes, quarters, half dollars

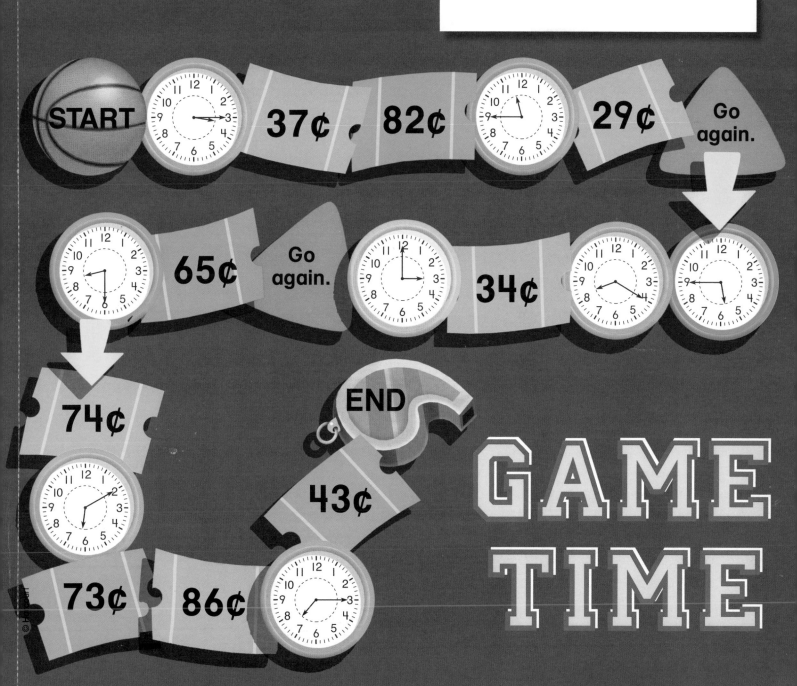

START 37¢ 82¢ 29¢ Go again.

65¢ Go again. 34¢

74¢ END 43¢

73¢ 86¢

GAME TIME

LOOKING FORWARD
SCHOOL HOME CONNECTION

Dear Family,

Today we started Unit 4. We will identify and use plane shapes and solid figures. We will explore congruence, symmetry, and moving shapes. We will describe, extend, and create patterns. Here is the math vocabulary and a list of books for us to share.

Love,

_____

Vocabulary

angle
edge
congruent

Vocabulary Power

angle

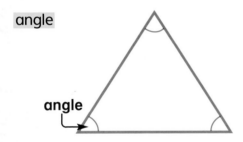

angle

edge

edge →

congruent Figures with the same size and shape.

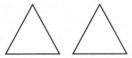

BOOKS TO SHARE

The Village of Round and Square Houses,
by Ann Grifalconi,
Little, Brown, 1986.

The Greedy Triangle,
by Marilyn Burns,
Scholastic, 1995.

The Quiltmaker's Gift,
by Jeff Brumbeau,
Scholastic, 2000.

Visit *The Learning Site* for additional ideas and activities. www.harcourtschool.com

Name _____

Algebra: **Sort Plane Shapes**

Vocabulary
side
angle
square corner
vertex/vertices

Learn

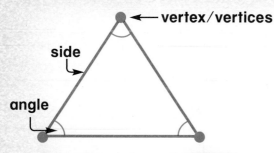
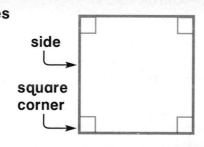

vertex/vertices
side
angle
side
square corner

A square corner is a special kind of angle.

This shape has 3 sides, 3 angles, and 3 vertices.

This shape has 4 sides and 4 square corners.

Check

Cross out the shapes that do not belong.

1. shapes with **more than 3 vertices**

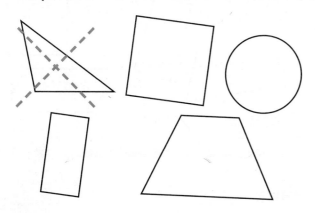

2. shapes with **no square corners**

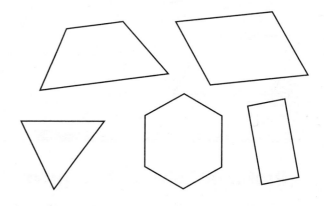

3. shapes with **more than 3 sides**

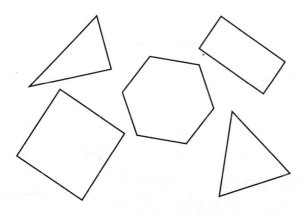

4. shapes with **more than 3 angles** and **more than 3 vertices**

Explain It ● Daily Reasoning

Why did you cross out the circle in Exercise 1?

© Harcourt

Practice and Problem Solving

Plane shapes can have sides, angles, vertices, and square corners.

Write a title for each group of plane shapes.

1. _____

_____

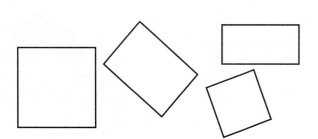

2. _____

_____

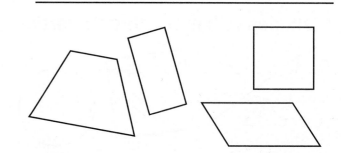

3. _____

_____

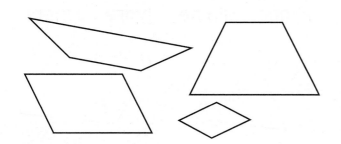

4. _____

_____

Problem Solving • Logical Reasoning

Write **true** or **false** for each sentence.

5. A square has 4 sides and 3 angles. _____

6. A trapezoid has 4 sides and 4 angles. _____

7. A parallelogram has 4 sides and 4 angles. _____

8. A circle is a curved shape. _____

 Write About It • Write about a shape, describing its sides, angles, and vertices. Trade papers with a classmate, and draw each other's shapes.

 **HOME ACTIVITY •** Make up sentences similar to those in Exercises 5–8 above. Have your child tell whether the sentences are true or false. Have your child correct the false sentences.

© Harcourt

Name _____

Extra Practice

1. Color the squares orange.

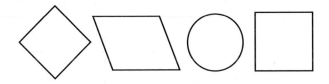

2. Color the rectangles blue.

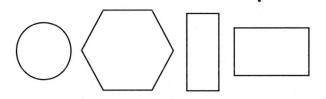

Write a title for each group of plane shapes.

3. _____

_____

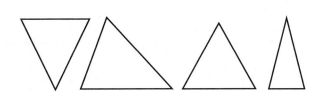

4. _____

_____

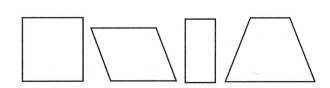

Place pattern blocks on top of the shape.
Draw lines inside the shape to show what shapes
you put together.

5.

6.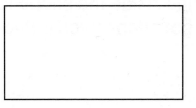

Problem Solving

Use pattern blocks. Make and
draw a model to solve.

7. Max drew a hexagon. He wants to cut
it into triangles. How many triangles
can he cut from the hexagon?

_____ triangles

© Harcourt

Name _____

✔ Review/Test

Concepts and Skills

1. Color the circles yellow.

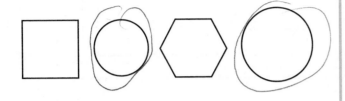

2. Color the trapezoids green.

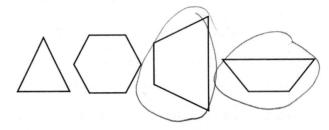

Write a title for each group of plane shapes.

3. _____

_____

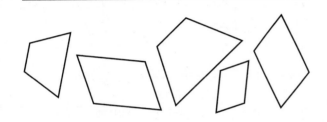

4. _____

_____

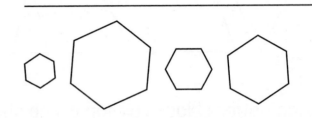

Place pattern blocks on top of the shape.
Draw lines inside the shape to
show what shapes you put together.

5.

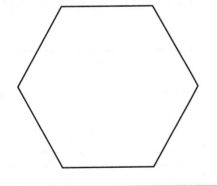

6.

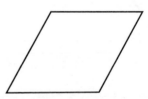

Problem Solving

Use pattern blocks. Make and draw
a model to solve.

7. Marie put 2 triangles together.
   What shape did she make?

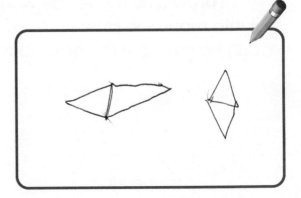

⭐ Standardized Test Prep
Chapters 1–18

Choose the best answers for questions 1–5.

1. Which color cube is most likely to be pulled from the bag?

- ○ red
- ○ blue
- ○ yellow
- ◉ green

2. What number is 10 more than 62?

52	63	72	82
○	○	◉	○

3. Neil made a model to find out what shape he could make by placing two squares together side-by-side. What shape did he make?

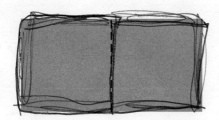

- ○ hexagon
- ○ triangle
- ○ circle
- ○ rectangle

4. What is the missing addend?
$8 + \underline{8} = 16$

7	8	9	10
○	◉	○	○

5. Which is a title for this group of plane shapes?

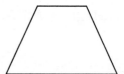

- ◉ shapes with 4 square corners
- ○ shapes with 3 sides
- ○ shapes with 3 angles
- ○ shapes with 4 vertices

Show What You Know

Choose the computational method to solve. Use paper and pencil or count back.

6.

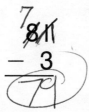

Explain why you chose the method you used.

You bobby l∉ slime

_____

_____

_____

MATH GAME

What's in a Triangle?
Take turns with a partner.

1. Spin the pointer.

2. Put 1 block of that shape on one of your triangles, if it fits.

3. The first player to completely cover both triangles wins.

You will need:

spinner

pattern blocks

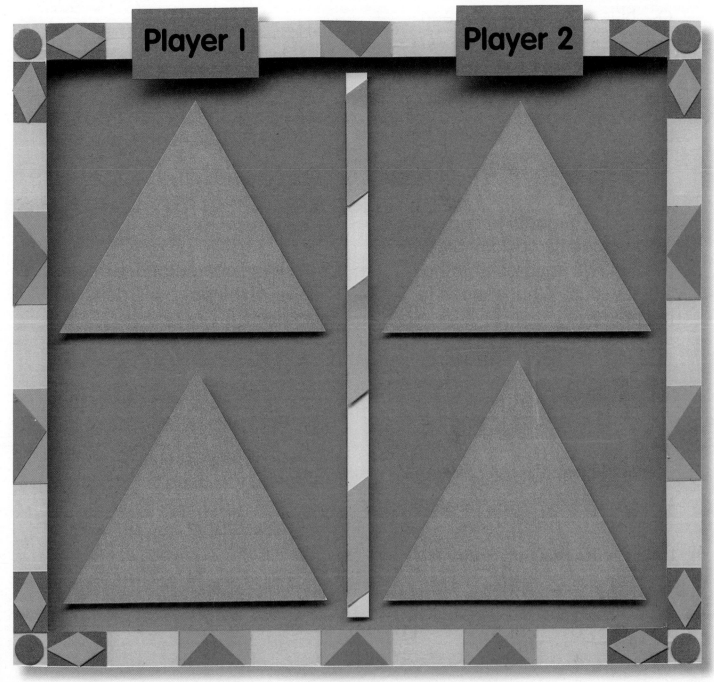

Player 1   Player 2

© Harcourt

Name _____

Algebra: Sort Solid Figures

Vocabulary
face
edge
vertex/vertices

HANDS ON Explore

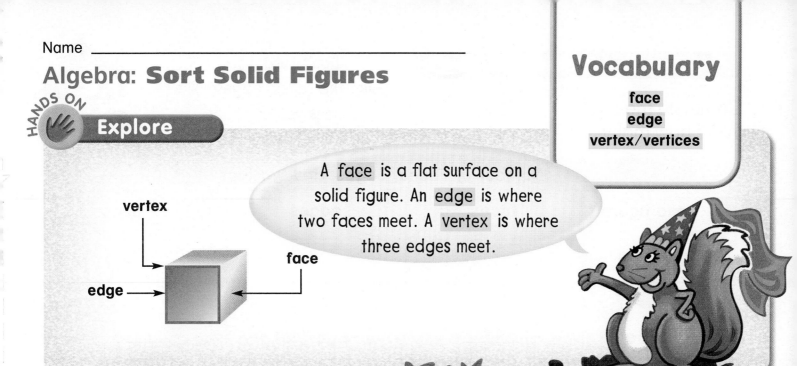

A **face** is a flat surface on a solid figure. An **edge** is where two faces meet. A **vertex** is where three edges meet.

vertex

edge

face

Connect

Use solid figures. Sort them by the number of faces, edges, and vertices. Color the correct figures.

1. 0 faces, 0 edges, 0 vertices

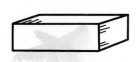

2. 6 faces, 12 edges, 8 vertices

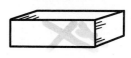

3. 5 faces, 8 edges, 5 vertices

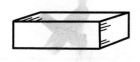

4. 6 faces, 12 edges, 8 vertices

Explain It ● Daily Reasoning

How are the cube and the rectangular prism alike? How are they different?

© Harcourt

Practice and Problem Solving

Complete the table.
Write how many.

Don't forget to count the faces, edges, and vertices you can't see.

Number of Faces, Edges, and Vertices

	solid figure	faces	edges	vertices
1.	cube	6		
2.	sphere	0	0	0
3.	pyramid			
4.	rectangular prism			

Problem Solving • Logical Reasoning

5. I am a shape with 4 faces that are triangles. I have 5 vertices. What shape am I?

_____

6. I am a shape with no faces, no edges, and no vertices. I have a curved surface. What shape am I?

_____

Write About It • Draw a pyramid and label the faces, edges, and vertices.

 HOME ACTIVITY • Gather objects from around your home that are shaped like solid figures. Have your child pick up each object, name the figure, and count how many faces, edges, and vertices it has.

Extra Practice

Color the figures that are the same shape.

1.

2.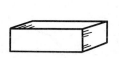

Complete the table. Write how many.

3.

Number of Faces, Edges, and Vertices			
solid figure	faces	edges	vertices
cube	_____	_____	_____

Use solid figures. Look at the faces.
Circle the solid figure you can make from the shapes.

4.

5.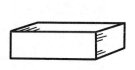

Problem Solving

Complete the table and solve.

6. Lila is making a cube. How many of each plane shape does she need to make the faces of the figure?

Number of Shapes Needed for Solid Figure			
solid figure	squares	rectangles	triangles
total			

Lila needs _____ squares, _____ rectangles, and _____ triangles.

Name _____

✔ Review/Test

Concepts and Skills

Color the figures that are the same shape.

1.

2.

Complete the table. Write how many.

3.

Number of Faces, Edges, and Vertices			
solid figure	faces	edges	vertices
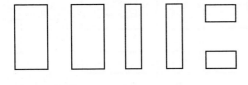 sphere	_____	_____	_____

Use solid figures. Look at the faces.
Circle the solid figure you can make from the shapes.

4.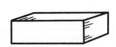

5.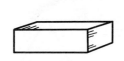

Problem Solving

Complete the table and solve.

6. Bradley is making a pyramid. How many of each plane shape does he need to make the faces of the figure?

Number of Shapes Needed for Solid Figure			
solid figure	squares	rectangles	triangles
total			

Bradley needs _____ squares, _____ rectangles, and _____ triangles.

⭐ Standardized Test Prep
Chapters 1–19

Choose the best answers for questions 1–3.

1. Which figure has the same shape as the one shown here?

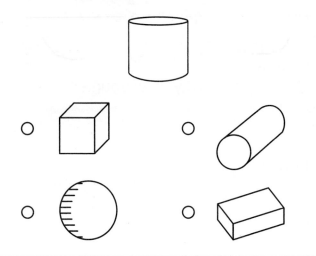

○   ○   ○   ○

2. How many faces, edges, and vertices are on a cube?

○   6 faces, 12 edges, 8 vertices

○   0 faces, 0 edges, 0 vertices

○   4 faces, 8 edges, 8 vertices

○   2 faces, 0 edges, 0 vertices

3. Which figure is a trapezoid?

○   ○

○   ○

Show What You Know
Make a bar graph to solve.

4.

Shapes in the Picture	
Shape	**Tally**
circle	III
triangle	⊬⊬⊬ I
square	II

TIP!

Color bars to show how many tally marks for each shape.

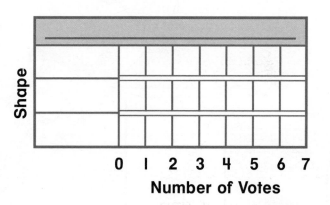

Shape

0 1 2 3 4 5 6 7
Number of Votes

Explain how the table and the graph show the same data.

_____

_____

_____

_____

STANDARDIZED TEST PREP

MATH GAME

Solid Castle

Play with a partner.

You will need:

spinner

12 red counters

12 yellow counters

1. Spin the pointer. Name the solid figure the pointer lands on.

2. Find an object in the room that is shaped like that solid figure. Choose a different object each time.

3. Explain how the object is shaped like the solid figure on the spinner.

4. Put a counter on a matching solid figure in the castle, if there is one not covered.

5. Take turns until all shapes in the castle are covered.

6. The player with more counters on the castle wins.

CHAPTER 19 • MATH GAME

© Harcourt

20 Spatial Sense

FUN FACTS

- In a mirror that curves in, your body will look very short. In a mirror that curves out, your body will look very tall.

- The world's largest mirror is in a telescope at the Paranal Observatory.

Using Data Is there a fun house in your city? Does it have fun house mirrors? Do research on the Internet or in your library to see what you can find out about fun houses.

© Harcourt

20

Name _____

✅ Check What You Know

Symmetry

Draw a line of symmetry to show two matching parts.

1.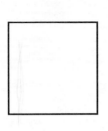

2.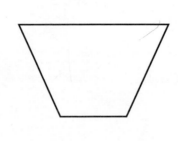

3.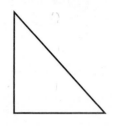

4.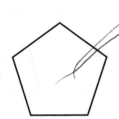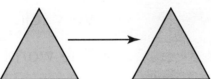

5.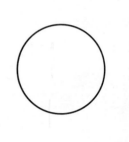

6.

Slides and Turns

Circle **slide** or **turn** to name the move.

7.

(slide)   turn

8.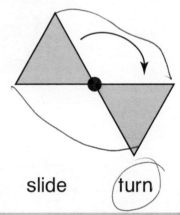

slide   (turn)

9.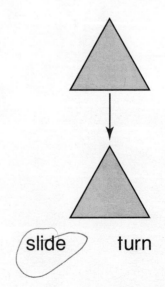

slide   (turn)

10.

(slide)   turn

344 three hundred forty-four   **Use this page to review important skills needed for this chapter.**

© Harcourt

Symmetry

Vocabulary
symmetry

HANDS ON

Explore

A line of symmetry divides a figure into two congruent figures.

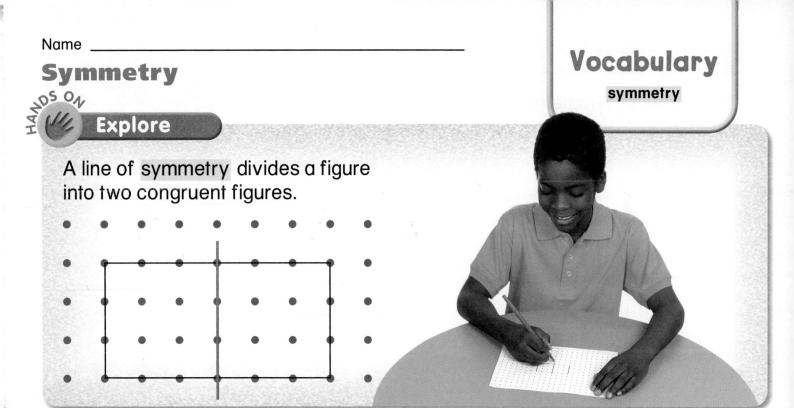

Connect

Copy the figure on dot paper. Cut it out. Fold the figure into two congruent parts. Draw a line of symmetry on this page.

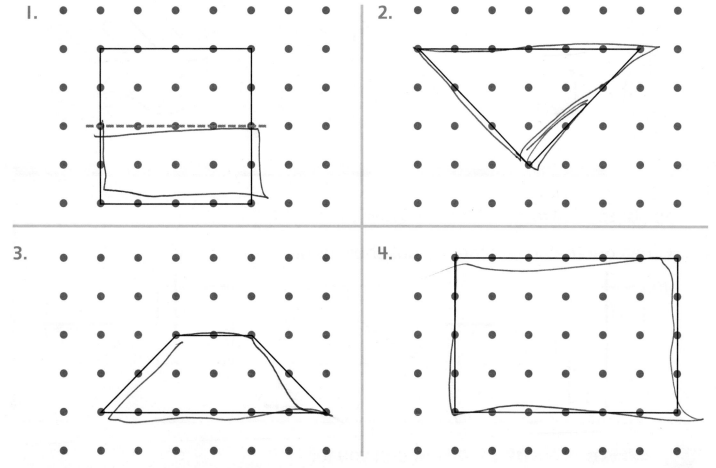

1.

2.

3.

4.

Explain It ● Daily Reasoning

How can you draw two more lines of symmetry in the square in Exercise 1?

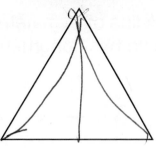

Draw a line of symmetry.
The two parts will be congruent.

1.

2.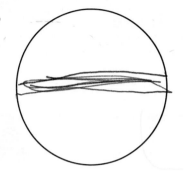

3.

4.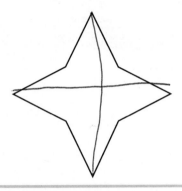

5.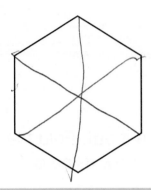

6.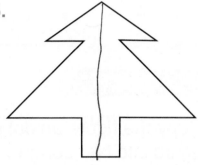

7.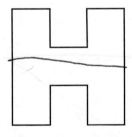

8.

9.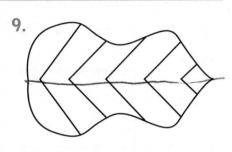

Problem Solving ● Visual Thinking

Cross out the figures that do not show a line of symmetry.

10.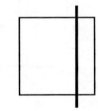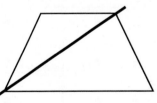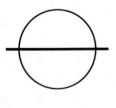

 Write About It ● How can you tell
whether a line is a line of symmetry?

🏠 **HOME ACTIVITY** • Have your child cut out figures and fold them to check for lines of symmetry.

Problem Solving Strategy
Predict and Test

Vocabulary

reflection

Nydia is playing a shape game. She looks at a
trapezoid and then at three other trapezoids in different
positions. <u>Which trapezoid shows a reflection?</u>

A reflection
looks like the
figure flipped.

UNDERSTAND

What do you want to find out?

Read the question. Underline it.

My test shows
that the reflection
looks like the
figure flipped!

PLAN

How will you solve the problem?

You can predict and test to find the reflection

SOLVE

Predict which trapezoid shows the reflection.
Underline it. Then place your mirror on the blue
line to test. Circle the letter of the correct figure.

A   (B)   C

Figure __B__ shows the reflection.

CHECK

**Check your answer. Does your
answer make sense?** Explain.

Problem Solving Practice

Predict which figure will show the reflection. Underline it. Then place your mirror on the blue line to test. Circle the letter of the correct figure.

Keep in Mind!
Understand
Plan
Solve
Check

1.

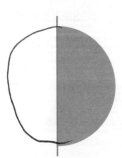 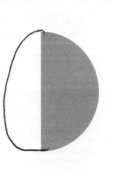 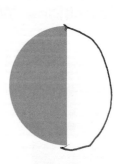

A   B   C

2.

 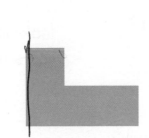  

A   B   C

3.

A   B   C

4.

A   B   C

🏠 **HOME ACTIVITY** • Draw and cut out a figure. Have your child use the figure to show a reflection.

352 three hundred fifty-two

© Harcourt

Name _____

Extra Practice

Are the two figures congruent? Circle **Yes** or **No**.

1.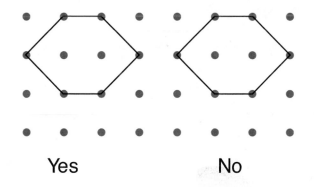

Yes   No

2.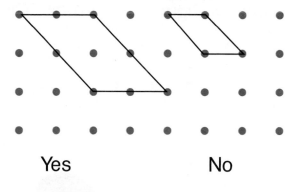

Yes   No

Draw a line of symmetry. The two parts will be congruent.

3.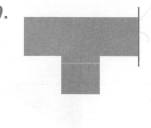

4.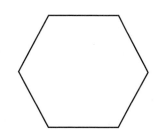

5.

Write the word that names the move.

6.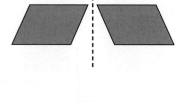

_____

7.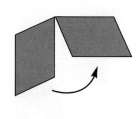

_____

8.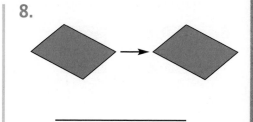

_____

Problem Solving

Predict which figure will show the reflection.
Underline it. Then place your mirror on the blue line
to test. Circle the letter of the correct figure.

9.

A   B   C

© Harcourt

Name _____

✔️ Review/Test

Concepts and Skills

Are the two figures congruent? Circle **Yes** or **No**.

1.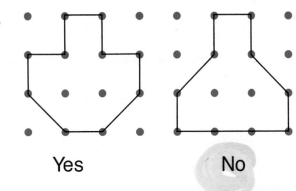

    Yes   No

2.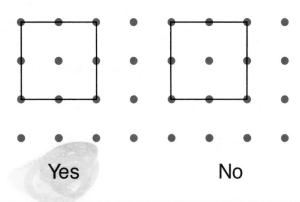

    Yes   No

Draw a line of symmetry. The two parts will be congruent.

3.

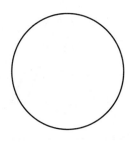

4.

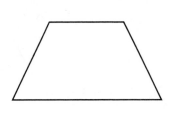

5.

Write the word that names the move.

6.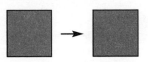

    _____

7.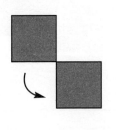

    _____

8.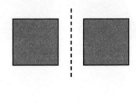

    _____

Problem Solving

Predict which figure will show the reflection.
Underline it. Then place your mirror on the blue line
to test. Circle the letter of the correct figure.

9.

   A   B   C

© Harcourt

Name _____

⭐ Standardized Test Prep
Chapters 1–20

Choose the best answers for questions 1–4.

1. Which word names the way the figure moved?

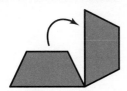

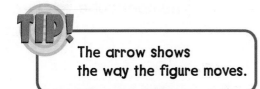

○ turn   ○ slide

○ flip   ○ square

2. Which figure is congruent to this figure?

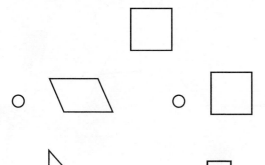

3. Which outcome is certain?

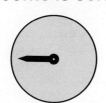

○ yellow   ○ red

○ orange   ○ green

4. Which figure shows a line of symmetry?

Show What You Know

Make a table to solve.

5. How many of each plane shape would you need to make the faces of 3 rectangular prisms?

Number of Shapes Needed for Solid Figures			
solid figure	squares	rectangles	triangles
rectangular prism			
rectangular prism			
rectangular prism			
total			

_____

Explain how the table helped you solve the problem.

_____

_____

_____

STANDARDIZED TEST PREP

Name _____

MATH GAME

Spinning Triangles

Take turns with a partner.

1. Put your 🔵 or 🔴 on START.

2. Spin the pointer.

3. Toss the number cube, and move that many spaces.

4. If the triangle you land on is congruent with the triangle the pointer points to, take another turn.

5. If the triangles are not congruent, your turn is over.

6. The first player to get to END wins.

You will need:

🔵 and 🔴

number cube 🎲 , 1–6

spinner

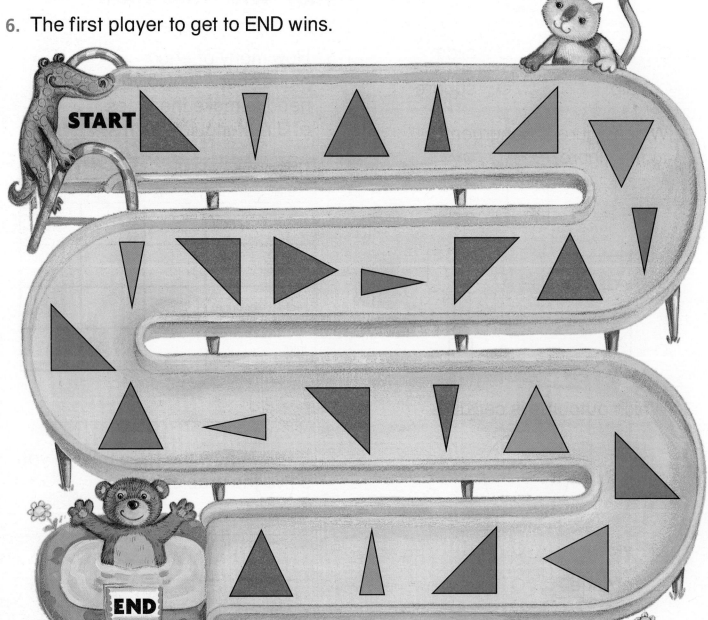

© Harcourt

FUN FACTS

- The largest piece of known kente cloth is about 12 feet by 20 feet.

- Kente cloth was first made by the Asante people in the African country of Ghana. It was worn only by kings, queens, and other important people.

Using Data Use bright colors and patterns to create a kente cloth.

Name _____

✅ Check What You Know

Describe and Extend Patterns

Find the pattern. Then color to continue it.

1.

2.

3.

4.

Pattern Units

Circle the pattern unit.

5.

6.

7.

Use this page to review important skills needed for this chapter.

© Harcourt

Name _____

Algebra: **Extend Pattern Units**

Learn

The pattern unit is orange elephant, purple whale, green turtle. The pattern unit helps you predict what comes next.

I know a purple whale comes next.

Check

Circle the pattern unit. Draw what comes next.

1.

2.

3.

Explain It • Daily Reasoning

How are the patterns in Exercises 1 and 3 the same?
How are they different?

THINK:
The pattern unit helps you know what comes next.

Draw and color to extend the pattern.

1.

2.

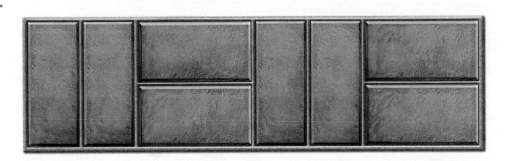

3.

Problem Solving • Logical Reasoning

Draw to extend the pattern.

4.

 Write About It • Look at the pattern in Exercise 4. Draw the tenth shape in the pattern. Explain what you did to find the correct shape.

⬠ **HOME ACTIVITY** • Create patterns with objects, and have your child continue the patterns.

Name _____

Algebra: **Make Patterns**

HANDS ON **Explore**

I used color and shape to make my pattern.

Connect

Use pattern blocks to make a pattern unit.
Repeat three times. Draw your pattern.

1. Use   .

~~~~~~

2. Use ▲ ▱ .

~~~~~~

3. Use ◣ ▲ ■ .

Explain It ● Daily Reasoning

How could you make a different pattern
unit with the shapes in Exercise 3?

Choose three pattern blocks to make
a pattern unit. Draw the pattern.
Repeat three times.

1.

Use the same three pattern blocks to make
a different pattern unit. Draw the pattern.

2.

Use the same three pattern blocks to make
a different pattern unit. Draw the pattern.

3.

Problem Solving ● Logical Reasoning

4. Toby made a pattern unit. He used a
   plane shape with 3 sides and a plane
   shape with no angles. Draw one
   pattern unit he could have made.

 Write About It ● In Exercises 1–3,
explain how your pattern changed each time.

🏠 HOME ACTIVITY • Help your child make patterns at home using objects, numbers, or pictures.

© Harcourt

Name _____

Problem Solving Skill
Transfer a Pattern

Ryan and Aneesa made the same
pattern in different ways.

Ryan made the pattern with pattern blocks.

Aneesa made the pattern by drawing flowers.

---

1. Tyler made a pattern with buttons.

Use letters to make the same pattern.

A   B   C   A   B   C   A   B   C

---

2. Danielle made a pattern by drawing pictures.

Use numbers to make the same pattern.

PROBLEM SOLVING

Show the pattern another way.

1. Andrew made a pattern with fruit.

2. Russell made a pattern with cards.

3. Lila made a pattern with shells.

HOME ACTIVITY • Create patterns with objects, and have your child draw pictures to show the same patterns in a different way.

366 three hundred sixty-six

© Harcourt

Name _____

Problem Solving Skill
Correct a Pattern

Layni made this pattern. She thinks she made a mistake. She finds the pattern unit. Then she corrects the pattern.

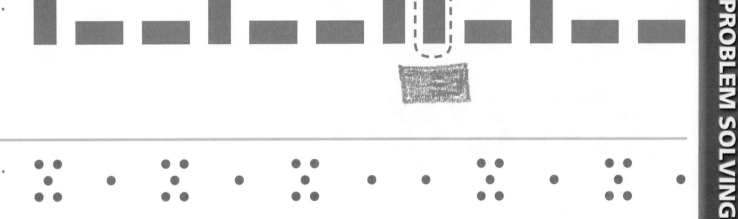

I left out the number 1.

Now the pattern is correct!

1 3 1 1 3 1 1 3 1 1 3 1

Read the pattern. Circle the mistake.
Correct the pattern.

1.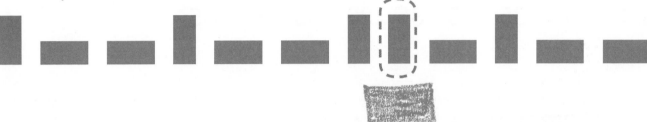

2. (braille dot pattern)

3. 4 6 8 4 8 4 6 8 4 6 8

4.

PROBLEM SOLVING

Problem Solving Practice

Read the pattern. Circle the mistake.
Correct the pattern.

1.

2.

3. 33   35   35   33   35   33   33   35   35

4.

5.

6.

HOME ACTIVITY • Create patterns with objects found around your home. Include an error in some of the patterns for your child to find and correct.

368 three hundred sixty-eight

Name _____

Extra Practice

Describe the pattern. Circle the pattern unit.

1.

_____

Circle the pattern unit. Write what comes next.

2.

2 I I 2 I I 2 I I 2 I I _____ _____ _____

Use ▲ ⟋ to make a pattern unit.
Repeat three times. Draw your pattern.

3.

Problem Solving

Show the pattern another way.

4. Nina made a pattern with crayons.

© Harcourt

Name _____

✅ **Review/Test**

Concepts and Skills

Describe the pattern. Circle the pattern unit.

1.

_____

Circle the pattern unit. Draw what comes next.

2.

Use  to make a pattern unit.
Repeat three times. Draw your pattern.

3.

Problem Solving

Read the pattern. Circle the mistake.
Correct the pattern.

4.

⭐ Standardized Test Prep
Chapters 1–21

Choose the best answers for questions 1–4.

1. Which comes next in the pattern?

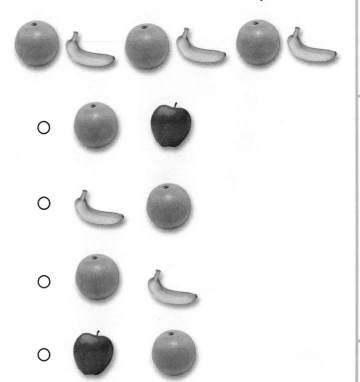

○

○

○

○

2. Which shows the pattern in another way?

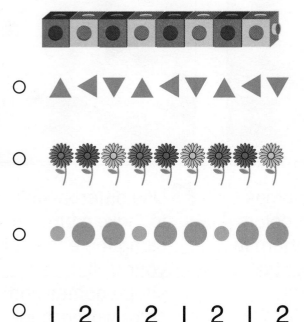

○ ▲◀▼▲◀▼▲◀▼

○ 🌼🌼🌼🌼🌼🌼🌼🌼🌼

○ ●●●●●●●●●

○ 1 2 1 2 1 2 1 2

3. Which number is greater than 75?

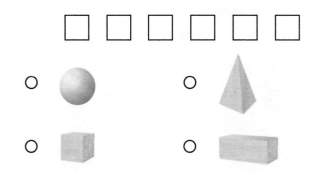

71   74   75   77
○   ○   ○   ○

4. Which solid figure has these faces?

☐ ☐ ☐ ☐ ☐ ☐

○ (sphere)   ○ (pyramid)

○ (cube)   ○ (rectangular prism)

Show What You Know

> 💡 **TIP!**
>
> The pattern unit helps you find the mistake.

5. Read the pattern. Circle the mistake. Correct the pattern.

• : • • : • • : • • : • •

Explain how you found the mistake and corrected it.

_____

_____

_____

_____

© Harcourt

IT'S IN THE BAG
Quilting Time

PROJECT Make a quilt as you name shapes and make patterns.

You Will Need

- Quilt (p. TR238)
- Construction paper
- Shape stamps
- Glue
- Scissors
- Ink pads (different colors)
- Markers or crayons

Directions

1 Cut out the quilt square and glue it to the construction paper.

2 Use shape stamps and different colors to make a pattern to decorate your quilt.

3 Use different colors to make a pattern along the edges of your quilt. Use shape names and color words to tell about your patterns.

Mrs. Quigley's Quilt

written by Lucy Floyd

illustrated by Christine Mau

This book will help me review plane shapes.

This book belongs to _____.

A

The winter was very cold. Mrs. Quigley decided to make a nice quilt to keep her piglets warm. First, she cut lots of cloth squares. Then she laid out some squares on the table.

"Too many squares," said Mrs. Quigley. "I need some different shapes." She put some squares together to make rectangles for her quilt.

How many rectangles did she make?

_____

C

"I think I'll add some little skinny shapes," said Mrs. Quigley. She cut some squares in half to makes skinny rectangles for her quilt.

How many skinny rectangles did she make?

_____

D

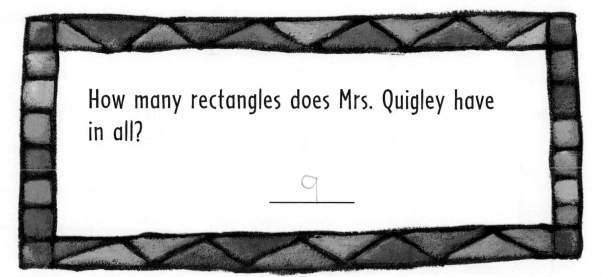

How many rectangles does Mrs. Quigley have in all?

_____9_____

E

"I need just one more shape," said Mrs. Quigley. She cut some squares in half to make triangles for her quilt.

F

How many triangles does Mrs. Quigley have?

_____

G

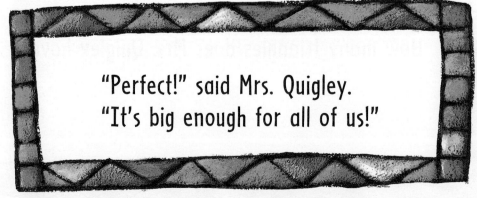

"Perfect!" said Mrs. Quigley.
"It's big enough for all of us!"

Name _____

PROBLEM SOLVING ON LOCATION

At the Beach

Jones Beach State Park is one of the most famous beaches in the world. It has more than 6 miles of beautiful beach. People can swim, surf, play in the sand, and watch everything from sea birds to starfish.

1 Draw a rectangle. Then draw its lines of symmetry.

2 Draw a triangle. Draw the flip of the triangle.

3 Use the following plane shapes to draw a sand castle on a postcard from Jones Beach.

Hello from Jones Beach!

Name _____

CHALLENGE

Solid Figures

You can put solid figures together to make different solid objects.

 and   and  make

Circle the solid figures that make each solid object.

1.  |

2.  |

3.  |

4.  |

Explain It • Reasoning

Explain why you could not place a cube on top of a pyramid.

374 three hundred seventy-four

© Harcourt